Teaching Violin to the Very Young Child, Vol. Two

By Jennie Lou Klim

Teaching Violin to the Very Young Child, Vol. Two is a sequel to Vol. One, and introduces the student to the notes on the A string, beginning with the 1st finger at the nut. This pattern, with the 3rd and 4th fingers close together, is easier and more natural for the small hand.

Overview of Vol. Two

- In Part 1, the child reviews the violin and bow hold, and plays the notes of the Bb Finger Pattern, with rote imitation.

- In Part 2, the child reads each note on the page as a word: open, one, two, three, or four. During this time, there is no playing.

- In Part 3, the child plays the music with the understanding of each note as a number, not a letter name.

<u>Part 1 Review</u>

The Violin Hold

The child places the left hand on the right shoulder, bringing the left shoulder to the front in such a way as to create a ledge on which the violin rests. The violin is placed on the shoulder with the jaw resting comfortably in the chin rest. The left hand returns to the fingerboard with the left elbow positioned under the violin. The forearm is turned in such a way so the four fingers are in line with the strings over the fingerboard.

Since the violin tends to slip, a cloth, sponge, or shoulder rest may be needed to create the friction that eliminates this slipping.

The Bow Hold

The right hand thumb is positioned between the hair and the stick, with the back of the thumb resting very gently on the hair.

The next three fingers are curved and placed around the bow stick, angled slightly toward the stick.

The tip of the little finger sits on top of the stick. There is an equal distance between the fingers. To ensure a relaxed hold, lift and tap each finger on the bow stick, one at a time.

Rote Playing with the Bb Major Finger Pattern

An introduction to playing is best done by learning the finger pattern, by rote in the first few lessons. The first finger is placed back to the nut for the beginning of the finger pattern that will be used throughout this book. They will quickly hear this pattern as the beginning of a scale. (The notes on the E string were learned in Vol. One.)

It is best that all playing takes place in the upper half of the bow, with the right arm bending at the elbow. Encourage the student to keep the bow between the bridge and fingerboard and listen to the tone that is produced. It is never too early to develop the skill of careful listening.

Parental Involvement

Encourage one parent to attend lessons, take notes, be involved in the learning process, and be aware of the practicing skills that produce the best results. The most efficient parent-teacher is the one who is also a student in this process.

At the top of each of the following pages is a message to be read to the student. It will serve as a guide to reading or playing the music on that page.

It is impossible to overestimate the importance of the habits formed in the early period of training, which may directly influence the whole later development of the student, and determine the possibilities for all future playing.

Timing is Critical

Children mature at different rates. The insightful teacher will recognize the maturity and attention span during the first lessons. If there is resistance, it may be best to put the lessons on hold for a few months, before resuming. It is important that every lesson be a happy time for both the young child and the parent.

This book is dedicated to my mother who sat beside me every day as I practiced.

Part 2 Reading the Notes on the A String

The Open A

The note for OPEN A is located in the 2nd space.
Stand in rest position, and read the music on this page.

J. L. Klim

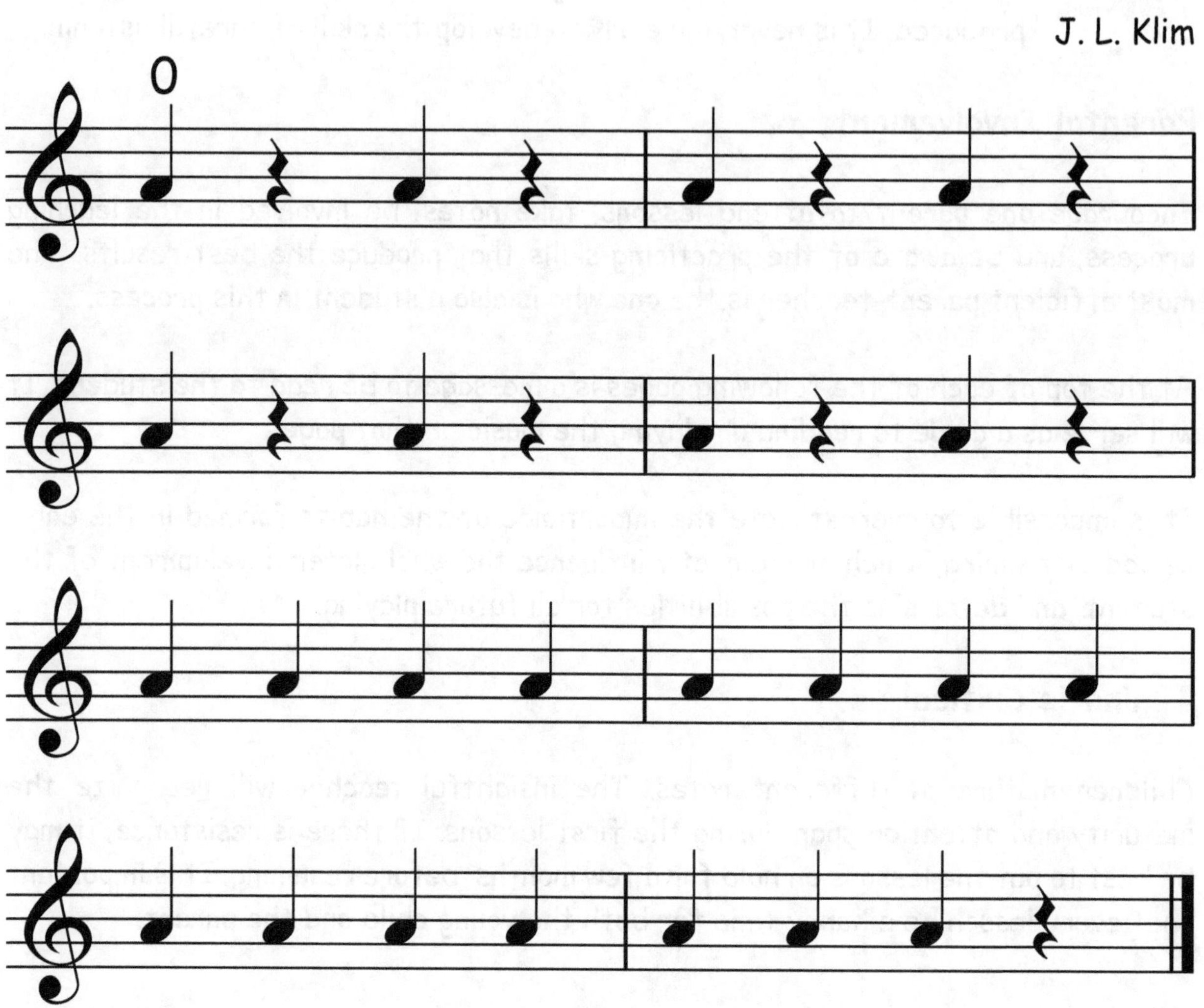

The Note - One

The note ONE is located in the middle line. Notice the flat sign beside it. Read these notes as OPEN and ONE.

J. L. Klim

The Note - Two

The note TWO is in the 3rd space. Read the notes as
ONE and TWO.

J. L. Klim

The Note - Three

The note THREE sits in another line. Read this music as
ONE, TWO, and THREE.

J. L. Klim

The Note - Four

In Book I, you learned that a note in the top space can be OPEN E. When there is a flat beside this note, it is can only be FOUR.

Reading Test

When you are confident with reading, you are ready to
move on, and play the next pages on your violin.

J. L. Klim

Part 3 Playing the Notes on the A String

The Open A

To begin, place your bow at the balance point, just below the middle,
Play in the upper part of the bow, bending your arm at the elbow.

J. L. Klim

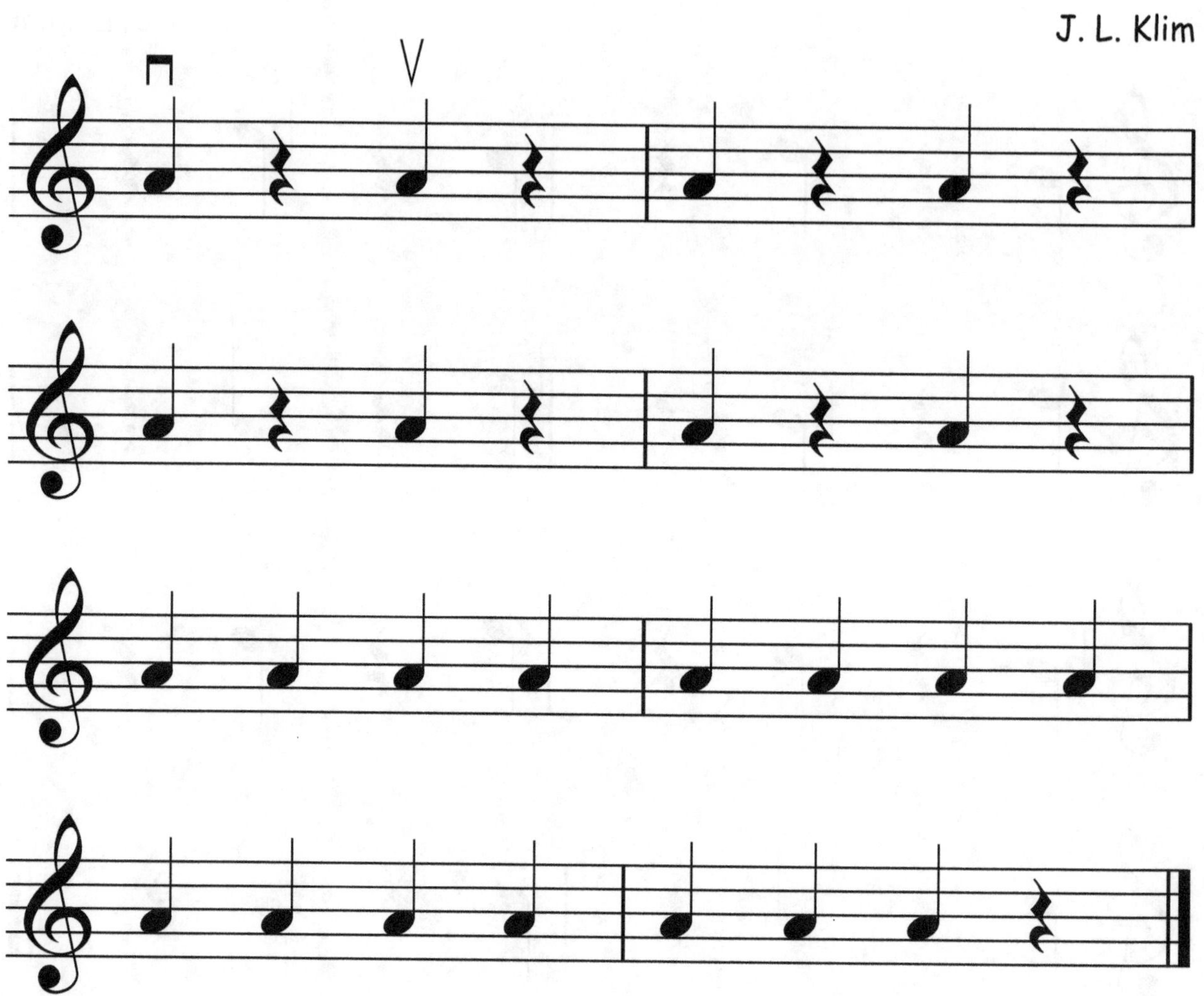

The Note - One

Notice the FLAT beside the 1st finger note. This requires the placement of the 1st finger to be back to the nut. There is a half step sound between the open A and the 1st finger.

J. L. Klim

The New Note: Two

The 2nd finger is placed one whole step away from the 1st.

J. L. Klim

The New Note - Three

The 3rd finger is placed a whole step away from the 2nd finger.
Keep the 1st finger down throughout this song.

J. L. Klim

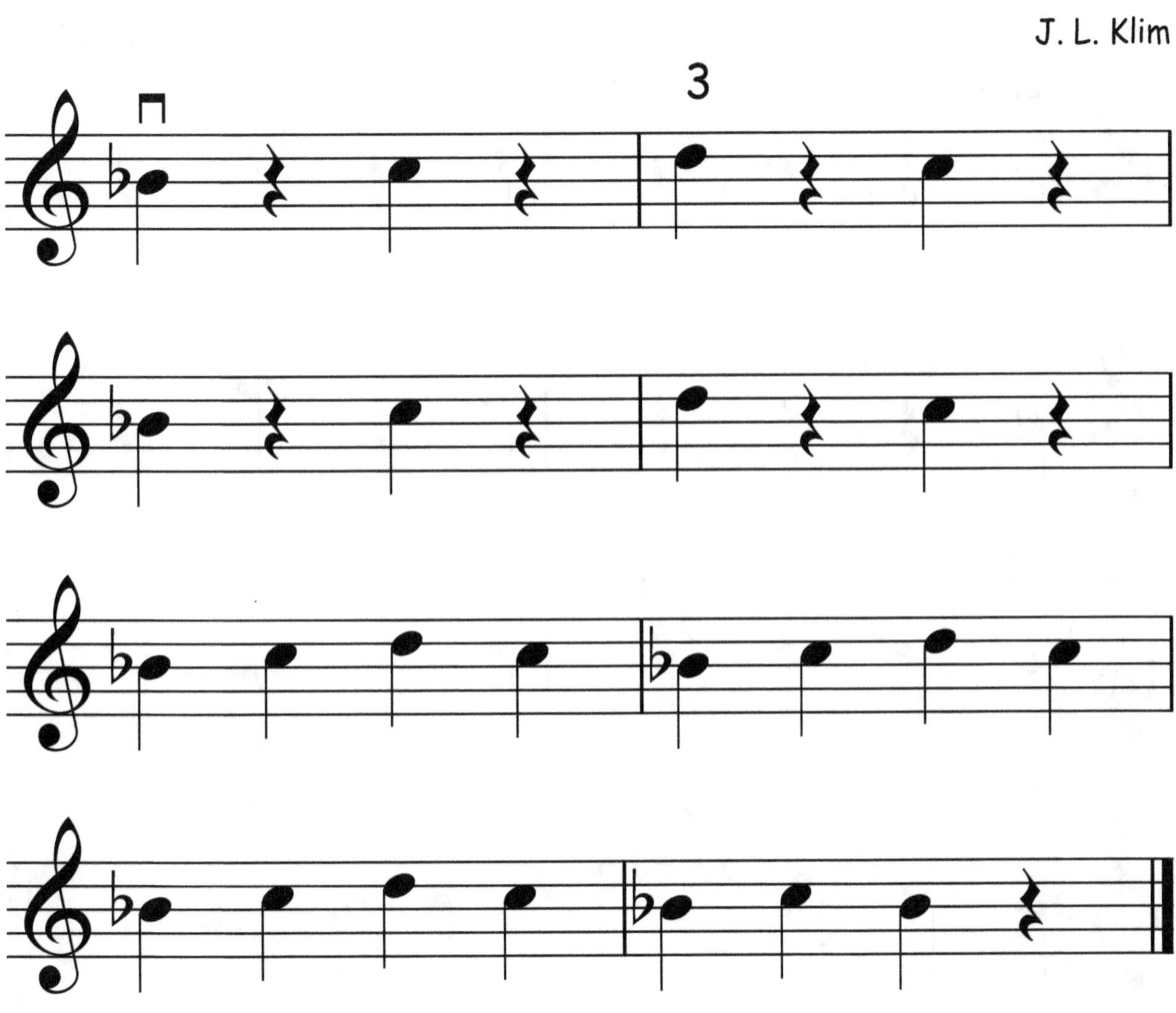

The New Note - Four

The 4th finger is placed close to the 3rd finger, because of the flat.
Notice, there are two flats in this pattern which is the beginning of
a new scale.

The Wind in the Trees

Keep the 1st finger down as much as possible.

Skippy, Skippy, One-Two-Three

You'll have fun with the skips, steps, and rests in this song.

A Fourth Finger Workout

Notice that the 2 flats are now located in the Key Signature.
The finger pattern is still the same.

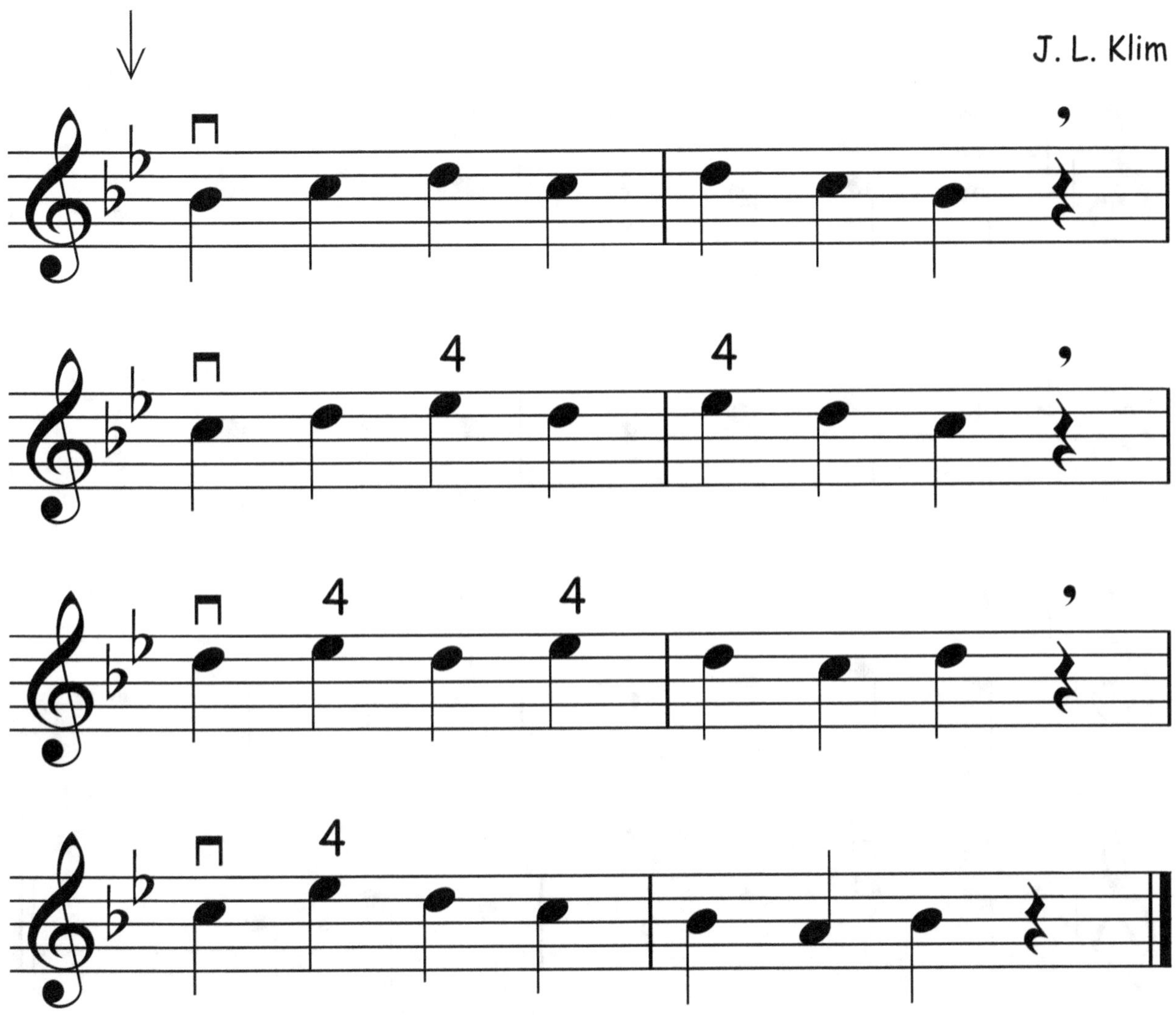

Let's Fly Through the Air

Say FLY as you return the bow to the balance point.

J. L. Klim

The Turtles

Notice the TIME SIGNATURE located at the beginning of the music. There are 4 beats in every measure. Each half note is worth 2 beats, and played with a longer bow.

J. L. Klim

Long Bows and Short Bows

Clap the RHYTHM before playing this song. Remember, the quarter notes are played with less bow.

J. L. Klim

More Long and Short Bows

Clap the RHYTHM before playing this song.

J. L. Klim

I Can Sing, I Can Dance

Remember to keep an even bow speed throughout this song.

J. L. Klim

Yankee Doodle

Remember to play the half notes with longer bows.

American Folk Song

Can you Follow Me?

Can you find the E string notes in this music? The finger pattern is the same on both strings.

J. L. Klim

Mary Had a Little Lamb

Here is the very familiar song, now played on the A and E strings.

English Folk Song

Crossing Strings

You learned to play eighth notes in Book I. Remember, they are played with less bow, NOT a faster bow.

Jingle Bells

Keep an even bow speed throughout this song.

J. Pierpont

A Snappy Tune

Keep your 1st finger down throughout this snappy tune.

This Old Man

You'll keep busy crossing strings and playing the shorter 8th notes, but you'll have great fun.

Nursery Tune

A Note With a Dot

The new note in this song is the DOTTED QUARTER note. It has 3 eighth notes hidden inside it. Clap this new rhythm with your teacher, before playing the notes.

Ode to Joy

Today is a joyful day. You can play on both the A and E strings, you have developed 4 strong fingers, and you have learned to play some wonderful music.